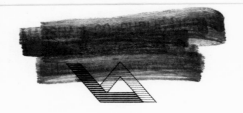

# THE PICTURE LIFE OF STEVEN SPIELBERG

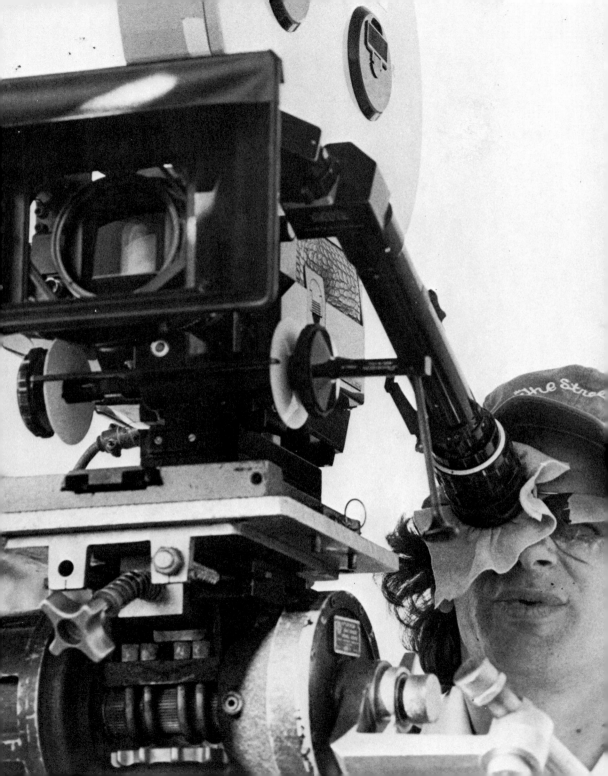

# THE PICTURE LIFE OF
# STEVEN SPIELBERG

## BY MICHAEL LEATHER

**FRANKLIN WATTS**
NEW YORK/LONDON/TORONTO/SYDNEY/1988

Cover photograph by M. Sennet, Shooting Star

Photographs courtesy of: Sygma: pp. 2 (Christian Simonpietri),
8 (Philippe Ledru), 17 (Nancy Moran); Pictorial Parade, Inc./
Fotos International: pp. 10, 12 and 54—top (Frank Edwards),
36; Phototeque: pp. 18, 25, 27, 28, 30, 32, 34, 37, 39, 43, 56;
Globe Photos: pp. 48 (R. Dominguez), 54 (bottom—Alan
Davidson); Starfile: p. 49; Ron Galella: p. 52.

Library of Congress Cataloging-in-Publication Data

Leather, Michael.
The picture life of Steven Spielberg/by Michael Leather.
p.    cm.
Filmography: p.
Includes index.
Summary: Presents the life and career of the filmmaker who directed
some of the most commercially successful movies in film history,
including "Jaws" and "E.T."
ISBN 0-531-10497-4
1. Spielberg, Steven, 1947-     —Juvenile literature. 2. Moving
-picture producers and directors—United States—Biography—Juvenile
literature.  [1. Spielberg, Steven, 1947-     . 2. Motion picture
producers and directors.]  I. Title.
PN1998.3.S65L43    1988
791.43'0233'0924—dc19

[B]
[92]

87-27992  CIP  AC

# CONTENTS

# THE PICTURE LIFE OF
# STEVEN SPIELBERG

# 1 CHILDHOOD

Peter Pan lived in an imaginary world called Never Never Land, where he never had to grow up. In a way, film director Steven Spielberg has followed Peter Pan's example, and movie audiences all over the world are happy he has.

"I have always felt like Peter Pan," he says. "I still feel like Peter Pan. It has been very hard for me to grow up."

It wasn't always easy for young Steven to make friends. His lively imagination was his steadiest companion. Later, when he began making films, he drew heavily on the daydreams and experiences of his childhood days. Many boyhood memories have found their way into his films, for example, memories of holding a thermometer to a lightbulb in an effort to fake illness so he could stay home from school (*E.T. The Extraterrestrial*), and of scary nights when storm-tossed trees outside his bedroom window seemed to come to life (*Poltergeist*).

*Many boyhood memories have become part of Spielberg's films. Here, he directs young Henry Thomas in* E.T. The Extraterrestrial.

Steven was born on December 18, 1947, in Cincinnati, Ohio. Arnold Spielberg, Steven's father, was an electrical engineer. He worked on early computer designs. He had to move several times to be near his work. While he was still a child, Steven, with his father, his mother, Leah, and his three younger sisters, Susan, Anne, and Nancy, moved from Ohio to New Jersey, then to Arizona, and finally to California.

Steven picked up his storytelling skills from his father, who often made up tales to tell Steven and his sisters. Along with the energy and creativity he inherited from his mother, a classical pianist, young Steven's imagination became a frightening thing, at least to his sisters. . .

Once, on a moonlit night, Steven stood outside the girls' window, making odd sounds and howling "I am the moon" while threatening to come inside and "get" them. Another time, he gathered the girls in their room to tell them that a pilot from World War II had somehow flown off course and ended up in their closet, where he had died. He told them that the flier had rotted there for twenty years. Of course, the girls didn't believe him—until they opened the closet door and saw the lit-up skull in a pilot's cap and goggles that Steven had planted there! Steven's vivid imagination was not always as appreciated then as it is today.

As a child, Steven was extremely messy. He didn't like to put things away in his room or hang up his clothes. His mother claims that his pet lizard, which once got out of its cage, was found alive in his room three years later! Steven also had eight pet parakeets. They lived on his curtain rod.

Steven's mother says that it wasn't always easy raising an energetic child like Steven. He was often full of mischief. Once, he cut off the head of his sister's doll and served it to her on a plate with lettuce.

The Spielbergs were Jewish. When he was twelve or thirteen, Steven had his *bar mitzvah*, which is a ceremony that prepares boys for their religious responsibilities as adults. Steven had to memorize a song called the *haftarah* and was supposed to recite it along with the elders of the synagogue. But he let them get ahead of him. That way, if he forgot something, he could just listen and pick up the words from them.

Even though they were religious people, the Spielbergs did not always follow all the customs of

*Spielberg kisses his mother at the annual Directors Guild Awards in March 1976.*

their religion. Both Steven and his mother loved lobster, but lobster is not kosher. (This means that it is against certain Jewish dietary laws to eat it.) Once, Steven was preparing to cook a lobster dinner for his family when the rabbi stopped by for an unexpected visit. Steven and his mother hid the live lobsters under Steven's bed, hoping the rabbi wouldn't smell them or hear their claws clacking.

Steven was not very interested in his school lessons, and school was not easy for him. For one thing, he felt out of place. He thought of himself as a skinny nerd and was often picked on by bigger kids. He was not good at subjects such as math, which he got through only because of his father's help. He was even worse at sports and failed gym three years in a row in high school.

There were very few Jewish people living in Steven's neighborhood in Scottsdale, Arizona. Kids passing by Steven's house would sometimes yell, "The Spielbergs are dirty Jews." But Steven knew who these kids were and where they lived. One night, he snuck out and spread peanut butter all over the windows of their houses.

By the time he was twelve or thirteen, Steven knew that making films was the career for him. His father had received a home movie camera as a gift. Bit by bit, Steven took control of it. He loved directing—setting up the action and supervising the actors. Before long, everything that went on in the Spielberg household was an opportunity for Steven and his camera.

His schoolwork suffered as a result of his strong interest in making films. Steven did not think that subjects such as math or science would help him with his directing career. He would rather make an 8mm film than do the assigned homework. Often, he would pretend to be sick on Mondays in order to edit the film he had shot over the weekend.

Steven also loved to watch television, but his parents were strict in choosing what he could and could not see. Whenever his parents were out for the evening, Steven would stay up until the babysitter fell asleep. Then he would tune in to all the forbidden late-night shows.

Although his interest in movies caused some problems, it also solved some. When Steven was thirteen, he was being bullied by an older boy at school. Steven was afraid of him, but he decided to try to win the bully over to his side. He asked him to play the lead role in a war film he was making. Then he dressed him up like a squad leader, in an army uniform with a helmet and equipment. By the time the bully had finished playing the role of hero in this film, he and Steven had become best friends.

Steven found subjects for his camera everywhere. He would often stage wrecks with his electric train set. His father didn't like this at all and threatened to take the trains away if Steven kept crashing them. So Steven filmed one last spectacular crash, so he could watch it again and again without causing damage.

At every family event, from carving the turkey to taking vacations, the action was captured by Steven and his camera. He would often get his mother or sisters to act in his projects. For war movies he made his mother dress up as a soldier and drive across the "set" (the setting, or where the action takes place) in the family Jeep.

Steven's father helped him build miniature sets. Mountains and other scenery were often made out of papier-maché.

When he was only thirteen, Steven made a forty-minute-long war film he called "Escape to Nowhere." This was quite an ambitious project, especially since he only had an 8mm camera to use. But the results were good enough for him to win first prize in a local film contest.

At sixteen, Steven made a feature-length 8mm movie (feature-length films are generally over an hour long), a science-fiction thriller called "Firelight." His sister Nancy played the lead role. She remembers him being very much a director in control. One scene called for her to look into the sun. "Stop squinting! Look up!" Steven would yell. The film turned out so well it was shown at a movie theater in Phoenix.

*Spielberg's experience with building miniature sets when he was just a boy has come in very handy in his career. Here, he is photographing a miniature set for the film* Raiders of the Lost Ark.

Shortly after this, Steven and his family left the Phoenix area for California, and his parents got a divorce. Even though they suspected it was coming, Steven and his sisters were very upset by the divorce. But Steven feels that his parents still did a fine job of raising him and his sisters.

Arnold continued to work with computers and to date has had twelve inventions patented under his name. Leah remarried and with her new husband, Bernie Adler, opened a kosher restaurant—no lobsters served—called "The Milky Way" in West Los Angeles. Steven's sister Nancy eventually moved to New York and currently works in the jewelry business. His sister Susan is now a homemaker and mother and lives in Maryland. Anne, like Steven, felt the lure of the film industry and is currently a screenwriter in Los Angeles.

*Spielberg's sister Nancy remembers her brother always being very much the director, always firmly in control of the action.*

# 2 A HOBBY BECOMES A CAREER

Steven stayed in California after his parents' divorce, to be near the motion-picture industry. When he was seventeen, he went on a tour of the Universal Pictures studio and lot and snuck away from the tour bus. The main group wasn't stopping at the sound stages, and that was where he most wanted to go. Sound stages are large open spaces inside soundproof buildings, where sets are built and where actors are actually filmed performing their roles.

While wandering around on his own on the Universal grounds, he met Chuck Silvers, who was head of the editing department. Steven explained his interest in film to Silvers, and Silvers told him he would like to see some of the films that Steven had made. The young director was thrilled. Here was someone actually in the movie business who wanted to see his work!

He was given a pass and returned the next day. After watching his films, Silvers told Steven he was very impressed. He encouraged him to keep on working but warned him that it was not easy to make it in the film industry.

But Steven now had a taste of the big time. The people at Universal were doing the work he wanted to do. This was where he wanted to be. So he started coming to the Universal lot every day that he could. Dressed in a suit and carrying a briefcase (full of lunch), he had no trouble passing the gate guard. He soon found an office that wasn't being used and took it over. He even bought a set of plastic letters and put his name into the building directory! During the time spent at Universal, Steven got many chances to talk to and learn from the directors, writers, editors, and others who were working there.

Steven enrolled at California State University, Long Beach, but he continued to spend time at the Universal lot. He tried to get the professionals there to look at his work, but there was a problem. His films were shot using 8mm film, with no sound. This is what amateurs use to make home movies—suitable for showing on office walls perhaps but not on a theater screen. Steven wanted his films to look more professional.

At that time 16mm film was being used by student filmmakers and some professionals. It has more room on every frame, which results in a picture of better quality. The equipment is more sophisticated, too, allowing for special effects such as zooms, dis-

solves, and fade-outs. It can also be used to make pictures with sound, and the projection equipment that runs it is of higher quality than that used with 8mm film.

However, 16mm film and equipment is very expensive, so Steven went to work in the college cafeteria to earn money for film and to rent a camera. Through his hard work and persistence, he was able to earn the money for the equipment and to make five short films while attending California State University.

In 1969, a friend who wanted to be a producer raised $10,000 for Steven to make a film. Producers put together "packages." That is, they find scripts, or screenplays (stories written specifically for theater or film), and match these up with directors. Then they provide the money to complete the project. Steven wrote and directed a short film called *Amblin'*, which was about a boy and a girl who hitchhiked from the desert to the Pacific Ocean. It took only ten days to shoot the entire film.

Using the connections he had made at Universal Studios, Steven showed *Amblin'* to various people there. It got a lot of attention. Later, it was even shown at the Venice and Atlanta film festivals. This was not just another home movie. Here was some fresh, young talent!

The head of T.V. production at Universal, Sidney Jay Sheinberg, wasted little time getting in touch with Steven. He offered him a seven-year contract to direct television shows.

Steven hadn't been able to get into film school, as directors George Lucas and Francis Ford Coppola had. He did his filming on the side, while he studied English in college. Now he could quit school and start his professional career immediately, without having to pursue a degree at all. It was a dream come true for the twenty-one-year-old filmmaker.

# FAME AND SUCCESS

Spielberg began his career by directing episodes of existing TV shows. He directed segments of the series "Columbo" starring Peter Falk. He also worked on "Marcus Welby, M.D." and on the show "Night Gallery," with Rod Serling from the original "Twilight Zone" series. Each episode of "Night Gallery" was a collection of three or four individual short, often scary, stories. Once, the young Spielberg got to direct Joan Crawford as a blind millionairess in an episode. Working on this type of show, called an anthology, would have a great influence on Spielberg and his later projects.

Eventually, Spielberg started directing movies for television. The first of these was *Duel*, starring Dennis Weaver. In it, a man in a car is pursued by a truck, the driver of which he never sees. This movie was shown both in the United States and in Europe. After this first effort, Spielberg did two more movies for television in 1972, *Something Evil* and *Savage*.

*Sugarland Express*, with Goldie Hawn, was

*Dennis Weaver leaps out of the way
of an onrushing truck in* Duel.

made in 1973 and was the first feature film directed by Spielberg. It was an action-packed movie with an exciting car-chase scene. While scouting (looking for) locations for the picture in Jefferson, Texas, Steven and his crew stayed for a time in a "haunted" hotel. The strange noises so unnerved them that they left to find a room in another hotel.

Spielberg had gotten more than just storytelling ability from his father. Some of Arnold's love of engineering and technology had rubbed off, too. Beginning with *Jaws* in 1975, Spielberg would make technology part of his film repertoire.

The title character of *Jaws* was a giant mechanical shark nicknamed "Bruce" by the crew. *Jaws* climbed to number five on the all-time box-office gross list. This meant that only four other movies had made more money than *Jaws*. Moviegoers clearly liked the idea of a small seacoast resort town being terrorized by a giant shark. It was frightening and entertaining.

The film was so popular that several sequels (films based on the same idea and characters) were made. However, Spielberg had no part in these, and they were not as successful as the original.

Spielberg had proven that he could make commercially successful films. But he didn't want to do the same kind of film over and over. Although he always kept his interest in technology and used spe-

Lou Jean Poplin, played by Goldie Hawn, holds a 12-gauge shotgun on the highway officer she helped to kidnap in Sugarland Express.

cial effects unsparingly to express his ideas, his subject matter changed significantly with each new project, even when he was doing sequels to successful movies.

After Bruce the shark came friendly, intelligent visitors from outer space in 1977 with *Close Encounters of the Third Kind*. This film starred Richard Dreyfuss, who had also starred in *Jaws*. (Many top directors use the same lead actors again and again.) *Close Encounters* represented a new turn in science fiction films. It was one of very few that depicted aliens as friendly and not determined to conquer the earth. The special effects were dazzling and included swift-moving "scout" ships and a huge, colorful, tinker-toylike "mothership." Steven even got to use Jiminy Cricket's song "When You Wish Upon a Star" in his

Above: *"Bruce," the giant mechanical shark from* Jaws, *terrorizes beachgoers and swimmers in a quiet Long Island resort town. The town's chief of police and his wife huddle anxiously over their son as the killer shark moves away.* Below: *Spielberg relaxes aboard the set, a vintage fishing boat, with three of the stars of* Jaws, *Robert Shaw (left), Roy Scheider, and Richard Dreyfuss (bearded).*

film, a sentimental favorite of his. However, it was cut from the original version and only shows up in the special longer edition of the film, which was released three years later.

Two years after *Close Encounters*, Spielberg directed a comedy called *1941*, written by the young team of Robert Zemeckis and Bob Gale. For special effects, the film featured a ferris wheel rolling off a pier, an exploding house, and a divebomber that strafes Hollywood Boulevard.

Even though such familiar faces as Dan Aykroyd and John Belushi (from television's very popular "Saturday Night Live" show) appeared in *1941*, the film did not do well at the box office. It had been very expensive to make, and Spielberg lost a lot of money. People were surprised that such a successful director could have a "flop." But Spielberg knew he would be taking a risk by making a comedy about the bombing of Pearl Harbor. In addition, he had never directed comedy before. He discovered that it wasn't his strong point.

Above: *Richard Dreyfuss, as Roy Neary, is shaken after a close encounter with a UFO in* Close Encounters of the Third Kind. Below: *the "mothership" in* Close Encounters

But this setback did not stop him. In 1981 he joined with another young filmmaker, George Lucas, to create the huge box office hit *Raiders of the Lost Ark* (Lucas had previously done *American Graffiti* and *Star Wars*). The story concerned an archaeology professor turned adventurer who travels around the world trying to recover a lost religious artifact and avoid being killed by Nazis pursuing the same goal.

The original idea for the film was Lucas's. The original script was written by Lawrence Kasdan. Lucas and Spielberg together came up with ideas to add to the original script. Lucas produced the film and Spielberg was let loose to direct it.

In 1982, Spielberg went back to outer space, this time with *E.T. The Extraterrestrial*. While Spielberg was developing the idea for the film, the title changed several times. It started out as *Night Skies* and later it became *After School* and *A Boy's Life*. The story changed along with the titles. Finally, it became *E.T.* But people connected with the film continued to use the title *A Boy's Life* while the shooting was going on. This was done to fool the press. Spielberg wanted to avoid any premature comparisons with

*"Wild Bill" Kelso, played by John Belushi (left), is a gung-ho American pilot in Spielberg's 1941.*

In this scene from the movie Raiders of the Lost Ark, Harrison Ford (right) as archaeologist Indiana Jones (below) runs from a huge boulder rolling toward him. The special effects in Raiders were quite spectacular.

*Close Encounters.* He also did not want to reveal anything about the storyline or characters.

Audiences everywhere quickly fell in love with the small, lost traveler from another planet. The story of his efforts to find his way home and his relationship with a small, lonely human boy made the film the number one box-office hit of all time. In some ways the story resembled that of *The Wizard of Oz.* E.T. was like Dorothy, lost in a strange land (earth would seem strange to an alien visitor) and trying to get back home. Spielberg provided a few new twists to the popular tale.

*E.T.* was nominated for an Academy Award for Best Picture. It did not win. But Spielberg came up with an idea for a sequel, a story describing E.T.'s adventures back on his own planet. This became a book entitled *E.T.: The Book of the Green Planet.*

Spielberg followed *E.T.* with a short segment from *Twilight Zone: The Movie* (1983), then *Indiana Jones and the Temple of Doom* in 1984, another wild adventure using the same main character as *Raiders of the Lost Ark* (Harrison Ford as the daring archaeologist "Indiana" Jones). The film was a commercial success but was criticized for being too violent, as were several other Spielberg films, including *Gremlins*, which Spielberg later produced.

At this point, Spielberg decided it was time for a change. A novel by Alice Walker, called *The Color Purple*, told the story of a poor black family living in

*Drew Barrymore (Gertie) kisses
E.T. goodbye in the movie E.T.*

Indiana Jones and the Temple of Doom, *the sequel to* Raiders, *featured more exciting action-packed sequences and dazzling special effects, such as this wild ride through a mine tunnel. Below: in the Spielberg segment of* Twilight Zone: The Movie, *residents of a rest home are taught how to regain their youth.*

Georgia. Spielberg wanted to put the story on film. As a book it had already won the Pulitzer Prize.

Spielberg had already made five films that set box-office records, but this film wasn't about sharks, aliens, adventurers, or ghosts. Could he be successful in making a serious film like this?

He felt he could, and so did Alice Walker. He took a long time to finish it. Even though some of the actors playing lead roles had never acted before, they worked very hard. Whoopi Goldberg, a comedienne, and Oprah Winfrey, now a popular talk-show host, were praised for their touching performances.

The movie was a commercial success. Spielberg had made a serious movie geared for an adult audience. *The Color Purple* was nominated for eleven Academy Awards in 1986, including Best Picture. However, Spielberg was not nominated for Best Director. This decision was very controversial. Most of the time, the director of a very popular and successful movie that has been nominated for Best Picture is automatically nominated for Best Director. Some people suggested that the nominating committee was resentful of Spielberg's huge commercial success, refusing to equate it with artistic greatness. Others said perhaps he was too young.

But there was also a deeper criticism of Spielberg's directing style. Both *The Color Purple* and *E.T.*, some felt, openly manipulated the audience's emotions. It is fine for a moviegoer to feel sympathy for a

*Spielberg directs novice actress Whoopi Goldberg in* The Color Purple.

screen character, and every good director wants the audience to become emotionally involved with the character's life. However, Spielberg, while a master at producing feelings of sorrow, terror, or excitement, often lacks subtlety and merely pushes his audience into an emotional response. Many people feel that it takes more than just successfully evoking emotions to make a great movie.

In any case, *The Color Purple* did not win Best Picture. In fact, it didn't win in any of the categories for which it was nominated.

All the controversy over *The Color Purple* did not seem to discourage Spielberg, however. He had too much to do, too many movies still to make.

# ON TO PRODUCING

Spielberg likes to get totally involved in every phase of his film projects. He has directed some of the biggest hits in movie history, and he has developed the basic storyline for many of these films. He has worked closely with writers to prepare screenplays and has written some screenplays himself. *Close Encounters* and *E.T.* were his stories turned into scripts by writers he chose. It seemed almost inevitable that Spielberg would wind up producing films, too.

At first, he produced movies to give other Hollywood hopefuls a chance at success, for example, Robert Zemeckis and Bob Gale with *I Wanna Hold Your Hand* (1978). But he also used his role as producer to make more of his film ideas a reality, even those he didn't have time to direct himself.

Sidney Sheinberg, who was the first person to give Spielberg a job working in the movies, had become president of MCA, the company that owned Universal Studios. Sheinberg was a devoted friend of Spielberg's and an admirer of his work. He also liked the money Spielberg's ventures brought in. So he agreed to build, on the Universal lot, the headquarters for a new production company Spielberg was starting. The new company, named Amblin' Entertainment, had as its logo (symbol) a boy on a bicycle with the small alien E.T. in the handlebar basket.

Spielberg's new headquarters are quite different from the usual office building. In fact, they resemble a frontierland-style amusement park more than an office complex. The front of the building looks like an adobe fort. American Indian artifacts decorate the inside. There is even a pond stocked with fish, and a waterfall. Sheinberg has spared no expense.

All this suits Spielberg perfectly. The offices house a screening room (where the director and others view the first versions of the movie) that seats thirty-seven people. There is also a large kitchen in the complex where Spielberg goes most mornings to make a pan of *matzah brei* (scrambled eggs and *matzah*), a favorite dish of his. It is estimated that Sheinberg spent between $4 and $6 million on Amblin' Entertainment's headquarters.

The new setup has allowed Spielberg to handle several projects at one time. There are often filmscripts that he wants to see made into films but does not really want to direct himself. These he will produce. Movies such as *Poltergeist* (released in 1982, co-produced by Spielberg and screenplay and story idea by Spielberg); *Gremlins* (released in 1984, execu-

*Spielberg wrote the screenplay for and produced
Poltergeist, a story about a haunted house.*

tive producer Steven Spielberg, written by Chris Columbus); and *Back to the Future* (released in 1985, with Spielberg as executive producer, story written by Robert Zemeckis and Bob Gale) were not directed by Spielberg. He suggested script changes, picked directors, and got the money together. In July 1985, *Time* magazine did a cover story on Spielberg, calling him the "Magician of the Movies."

Some of Spielberg's many story ideas aren't complex enough for a full-length movie. Spielberg needed a different format for these. He decided to do a weekly television series called "Amazing Stories." Each episode would present a new story. NBC liked the idea so much that it gave Spielberg a unique contract. Most of the time, a network will only purchase six to twenty-two weeks' worth of shows. This time, it bought two years' worth (forty-four episodes) and paid a record-breaking $800,000 to $1 million for each show. "Amazing Stories" was very similar to the "Night Gallery" shows Spielberg had directed earlier in his career. It, too, was an anthology series. Each week a new story would frighten, or sometimes amuse, its television audience.

Spielberg hired some well-known people to direct different segments. Famous directors such as Martin Scorsese and Clint Eastwood were happy for the chance to work with him. But Spielberg also remembered how he had been given his first chance to direct when he was only twenty-one, so he decided to also use young directors from local film schools. And he searched for good scripts from young writers. In one episode of "Amazing Stories," Spielberg's mother, Leah, made an appearance.

Amblin' Entertainment and Steven Spielberg will be busy for a while. Although "Amazing Stories" was canceled, there are plans to continue both the "Indiana Jones" series and do a sequel to *Back to the Future*. Other movie projects are planned, both for Spielberg and for other people to direct. *Batteries Not Included* is the title of a recent project by Spielberg shot in a depressed New York City neighborhood in 1986. There was some controversy over this filming. The poor people of the area criticized Spielberg for exploiting them and giving them nothing in return. Spielberg did later make donations to some local groups trying to help the homeless and those people being forced out of their homes by greedy landlords.

Another new area of film in which Spielberg has begun to experiment is animation. Animation means giving life to lifeless objects, such as clay figures or cartoon characters, to make it seem as if they are alive. One Spielberg animated feature, called *An American Tail*, was released at the end of 1986. It tells the story of a family of immigrant mice who come to America on a steamship. Spielberg has plans for at least one more animation project, and perhaps a third later on.

# 5 OTHER INFLUENCES

Movies and television have been a magnetic force for Spielberg throughout his life. The moving images on the screen can hold his attention for hours. In fact, he started staging his own train crashes after seeing the circus train wreck in Cecil B. DeMille's *Greatest Show on Earth* (1952).

Walt Disney films were an early influence on Steven. They were among the few films his parents would allow him to see. When he first heard Jiminy Cricket sing "When You Wish Upon a Star," he wanted to make a movie based on the song. (You'll remember he tried to include the tune in *Close Encounters*.) Also on his parents' "approved" list was *The Wizard of Oz*.

Alfred Hitchcock was another favorite director of Spielberg's, but Steven had to wait until he was old enough to escape parental authority before he could see any of Hitchcock's work in the movies. He saw some Hitchcock pieces on television.

Hitchcock was known for his careful planning

before he ever got the cameras rolling. Each shot was storyboarded (a drawing of it was made), and all camera placements and actor movements were mapped out. It has been said that Hitchcock actually *made* the movie on paper and that shooting it was a mere formality.

Spielberg has often used the same technique, especially when planning his special-effects sequences. This way he could be sure to get all the footage he wanted, and he could also confirm that the special-effects crew was capable of making it all happen. Lately, he has used storyboarding less and less in order to allow for more creativity and spontaneity in the films.

Steven almost got to meet Hitchcock while *Sir Alfred* was filming *Family Plot* (1976) at Universal. *Jaws* was already a hit, and Steven showed up on the sound stage, hoping perhaps they could meet, director to director. But an assistant to Hitchcock told Steven that Hitchcock was afraid it would "disturb" him to have Spielberg watch him work. He asked him to please leave!

Spielberg has had better luck with his contemporaries. Film-school graduates such as George Lucas, Francis Ford Coppola, and John Carpenter all came to Hollywood at around the same time. They formed a sort of directors' "Brat Pack." Steven belonged to this newer generation of filmmakers, even though he

Above: *Spielberg with directors Martin Scorcese (right) and Brian DePalma.*
Right: *Spielberg with director George Lucas*

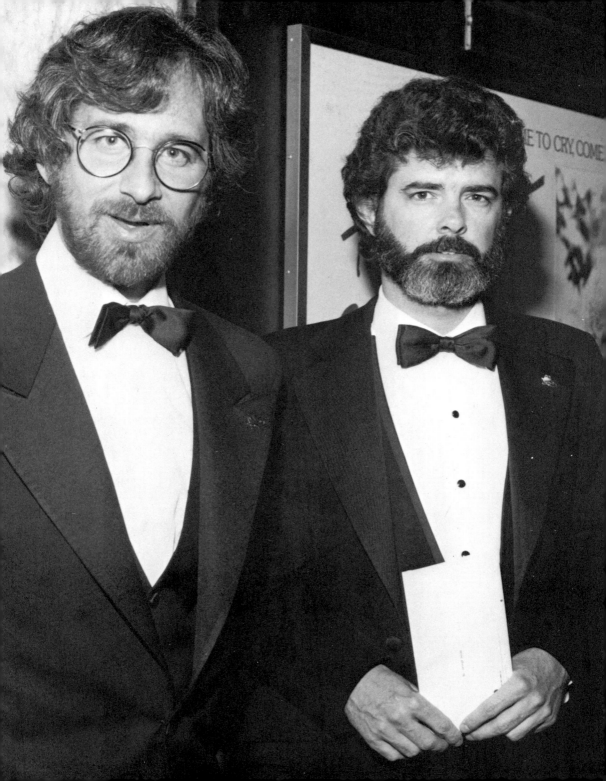

hadn't attended any of the well-known film schools such as the University of Southern California.

Spielberg collaborated with Lucas on *Raiders of the Lost Ark*. The idea was Lucas's, but Spielberg directed. The partnership started over a conversation about what kind of film each of them would like to do next if they could choose any film. Spielberg had always wanted to do a James Bond film. Lucas had an idea that was "better than Bond," and he also had his own company, called Industrial Light and Magic, to handle the special effects. Lucas had formed this company from some of the people who had worked for him when making *Star Wars*.

Spielberg apparently believes in film as a collaborative art. After his successful partnership with Lucas, he joined with four other directors to do *Twilight Zone: The Movie*. Spielberg has also been talking to Brian DePalma (director of *Wise Guys, Body Double,* and *Carrie,* among others) about two new film ideas. One is tentatively called *Congo* and the other *Starfire*.

# HONORS
# AND
# HOME LIFE

All of Steven Spielberg's hard work, creativity, productivity, and success was finally recognized by the Academy of Motion Picture Arts and Sciences. In March 1987, Spielberg was given the Irving Thalberg Award at the Oscar (Academy Award) ceremonies. The award honors an entire body of work.

It was truly a fitting reward for Spielberg. Both Spielberg and Thalberg were "wunderkinds," taking Hollywood by storm at a young age. Irving Thalberg was a legendary producer in the 1920s and 1930s at both Universal and Metro-Goldwyn-Mayer. He was only twenty years old when he was running Universal. Steven was not much older when he began his string of blockbuster hits. Both men are known for their enthusiasm toward their work. Both Thalberg and Spielberg recognized the importance of seeking out and nurturing new talent in the film industry. Unfortunately for the movie industry, Irving Thalberg died when he was only thirty-seven.

Spielberg is one of the youngest directors ever to win such an award. Most of the winners have been

directing for years and years and are in their sixties or seventies. Steven was just thirty-nine.

Before this, not one Spielberg movie had ever won an Academy Award in a major category. The only awards Spielberg had ever gotten for his work were in 1973, for his television film *Duel*, which won the "Grand Prix" at the Avoriaz Festival in France, and an award for Best First Film at an Italian festival.

Obviously, Spielberg loves his work and could keep himself busy with it twenty-four hours a day. But lately he has found time for a home life.

Amy Irving, an actress who has appeared in such movies as *Carrie, The Fury,* and *Yentl*, began dating Spielberg in 1975 but broke up with him in 1979. Then, in 1983, she was working on a film in India when she found out that Spielberg was arriving to scout locations for his film *Indiana Jones and the Temple of Doom*. She decided to surprise him at the airport. They began dating again and then moved in together.

On November 27, 1985, they were married in Sante Fe, New Mexico. Together they have "co-produced" a son, named Max Samuel. Playing with his

*Director Steven Spielberg accepts the Irving Thalberg Award at the Academy Awards presentations in March 1987.*

*Actress Amy Irving with Spielberg in September 1978*

*Max Samuel Spielberg with his proud parents, in March 1985*

son is now a favorite way for Spielberg to relax at home. He is a private person and does not actively seek the spotlight or interviews. He is happiest while working or being with his family.

Max should have plenty of stories to listen to as he grows up, as Spielberg shows no signs of running out of tales to tell. Max provides him with a whole new set of childhood experiences to draw upon. In fact, when Spielberg thinks of what projects to take on, he keeps in mind the types of films and television shows he would like Max to see. Perhaps following in the footsteps of his parents, Steven intends to monitor carefully what Max sees and thinks parents should take a more active interest in the kind of entertainment their children watch.

Steven Spielberg is one of the most successful filmmakers of all time. Ideas come to him all the time, whether he wants them to or not. His work appeals both to children and to the child in adults that never grows up. He knows what fascinates us, what scares us, what secret wishes we have because *he* had, and still has, those same fascinations, fears, and wishes. And he uses his childhood daydreams and experiences as building blocks for his movies.

If there is such a place as Never Never Land, where Peter Pan lives and never grows up, then Steve Spielberg has captured the spirit of it in his films. Like in the story of Peter Pan, Spielberg's

movies often cast adult characters in the roles of dis-
believers or clumsy and inept authority figures. They
are excluded from the child's magical world because
they would ruin it. But we, as the movie audience,
are happily invited to enter. Perhaps Spielberg hopes
to save us from the film adult's fate, to help us hang
on to some of our childhood fantasies. By giving us
this glimpse into the minds and hearts of the young,
he may even hope to help us grow up.

*Spielberg knows what fascinates us,
for they are the things that fascinate
him. Here, a favorite character of his
from boyhood, the fictional Sherlock
Holmes, becomes a character in a
movie he produced,* Young Sherlock
Holmes *(released 1985).*

# GLOSSARY OF FILM TERMS

*Animation.* The filming of non-moving drawings, puppets, clay figures, or other objects one frame at a time, with slight adjustments made in their pose or position. Running these drawings quickly in succession creates the illusion of movement.

*Anthology.* A collection of stories, poems, etc. A film anthology is made up of several separate segments. A television anthology series presents a different story each show.

*Dailies.* Developed prints of the film shot the day before. Viewing the dailies allows the director working on a movie to check his or her work and see if the shots that were needed came out all right.

*Director.* The person who has the most control over the shooting of a film. Directors often supervise not only the actual filming but also the casting of actors and the editing of the film and script itself.

*Dissolve.* Gradually exposing a new image over the existing screen image while the existing image is slowly fading away.

*8mm, Super 8mm.* Amateur and home movie film format. The term 8mm refers to the width of the filmstrip.

*Fade-in/out.* A fade-in is the gradual emergence of a scene from blackness to full clarity. A fade-out is the opposite.

*Feature (-length) film.* Any fictional entertainment movie that uses more than 3,000 feet of film (about thirty-four minutes). Modern-day features, however, usually run for an hour or more.

*Movie editor.* A person who takes all the scenes and individual shots the director has filmed and assembles them along with the music and other sound tracks into the final print of the film.

*Producer.* The one in control of the money in the film world. He or she is head of all personnel, including the director. The project might originally be the producer's overall conception, but he or she usually delegates the artistic responsibilities in order to concentrate on the commercial (profit-making) aspects of a film.

*Rough cut.* Prior to a final edited version of a film an editor assembles a "rough cut" to see if all the chosen footage works together.

*Scouting (locations).* Searching for just the right house, town, street, or land on which to film (or that can be adapted to the film's needs) when shooting outside of the studio.

*Screening room.* A miniature movie theater that producers, directors, and film studios often have where they can view the day's footage or a rough cut of a film.

*Screenplay.* A play script that is written to be filmed. Looks much like a stage-play script, with a concentration on dialogue and story development.

*Screenwriter.* The person who writes the screenplay or adapts a book, stage play, or other work for film.

*Script.* See *Shooting script.*

*Sequel.* When a film proves immensely popular, another film using the same characters, setting, storyline, or situation is almost sure to follow. This is a sequel.

*Set.* The place where the actual filming takes place. It can be a crew-built studio set or a scouted location.

*Shooting script.* A story (screenplay) with technical information included, such as camera direction and breaks for individual shots. It is a technical manual for the crew.

*16mm.* A film format (wider than 8mm) used by students and in many documentary and training films.

*Sound stage.* A space specifically constructed for the filming of movies, television shows, or commercials. It consists of a large empty space with high ceilings equipped with a gridwork of metal pipes from which lights hang. Sets are constructed on the sound stage, which is soundproofed to aid in recording dialogue.

*Sound track.* In a film, everything that you hear is part of the sound track. It is made up of separate parts such as dialogue, music, and sound effects (i.e., gunshots, explosions, etc.).

*Special effects.* Any filmed action that cannot be achieved by directly shooting it, including dissolves and fade-ins/outs as well as more spectacular miniature model photography, laser blasts, and making actors fly. Special effects are produced by many different departments, including camera, make-up, sound, and props.

*Storyboards.* A panel made up of drawings of each individual shot or sequence in a film. Each drawing shows everything that is required in a scene from costume and make-up to camera position, effects, lighting, stunts, and props. Storyboards help the director to plan camera and actor placement, as well as serve as an aid in determining the action of a scene.

*35mm.* Professional film format. Feature films and made-for-TV movies are shot on 35mm.

*Zoom.* A specific type of lens that can make it appear that the viewer is moving closer to or further from an object or person. Zoom also refers to the action the lens performs, i.e., "zoom in" or "zoom out."

# FILMOGRAPHY

MADE-FOR-TV MOVIES
*Duel*, 1971 (released as a feature in Europe)
*Something Evil*, 1972
*Savage*, 1972

FEATURE FILMS AS DIRECTOR
*The Sugarland Express*, 1973
*Jaws*, 1975 (fifth highest grossing film of all time)
*Close Encounters of the Third Kind*, 1977 (fifteenth highest grossing film
  of all time)
*1941*, 1979
*Raiders of the Lost Ark*, 1981 (seventh highest grossing film of all time)
*E.T. The Extraterrestrial*, 1982 (first highest grossing film of all time)
*Twilight Zone: The Movie*, 1983 (segment director)
*Indiana Jones and the Temple of Doom*, 1984 (eighth highest grossing
  film of all time)
*The Color Purple*, 1985

FEATURE FILMS AS PRODUCER ONLY
*I Wanna Hold Your Hand*, 1978
*Used Cars*, 1980 (co-executive producer)
*Continental Divide*, 1981
*Poltergeist*, 1982
*Gremlins*, 1984 (seventeenth highest grossing film of all time)
*The Goonies*, 1985
*Young Sherlock Holmes*, 1985
*Back to the Future*, 1985
*The Money Pit*, 1986
*An American Tail*, 1987 (animated feature)
*Inner Space*, 1987
*Harry and the Hendersons*, 1987

FILMS AS WRITER ONLY
*Ace Eli and Rodger of the Skies*, 1973

# INDEX